You Have Always Been Here

Julie S. Paschold

𝄢

Bass Clef Books
Cecilia, KY

First Edition

ISBN

979-8-9898478-2-2

Bass Clef Books is an imprint of MARZEK Publishing
Mick Kennedy, Publisher

Cover Art

Untitled

Julie Paschold

Printed and distributed by
Lulu.com

9 798989 847822

Acknowledgements

Thank you to my parents, who taught me to love completely. Thank you to my children, Halla and Lyle, who taught me to love deeply. Thank you to my twin sister Amy, who taught me to love timelessly. Thank you to my recovery friends, who taught me to love myself. For all those who have stuck by me through everything, my unending gratitude. For my poetry pals and mentors, thank you for guiding my literary journey. Thank you to Bass Clef Books for giving this chapbook a chance to see the world. For that higher power out there, thank you for creating love to make this world a beautiful place to live.

Contents

You Have Always Been Here

To my twin Amy,

the first person I learned to love

I've Been Here Before

Walking in blue circles
the white line I follow meeting itself

again and again

I am trying to reconcile
these thoughts of you,

someone who has known me
every day of my life
it seems,

someone I had lost connection to
until my book created a bridge
that brought us together again,

my dream not so much a sexual fantasy
but more an amazement,

a certainty of destiny
at our new reunion,

and I am pondering now,
looking back at our separate journeys,

wondering if my scarred and tormented past
that has brought me humility
and an immense capacity to love

may somehow merge with yours,

if your years of solitude
have created someone
who does not allow another to love him, or

if you will stay and not run away
the closer we move toward each other,
the more we learn of each other,

if you will let me love you
in however form that develops,

because I have been here before,
this reaching for each other,

this growing close, but not with someone
who has known me every minute
I have breathed on this earth,

not with you,

so I trust somehow this dream
was telling me to reach out, to stop
walking in circles,

to find I am no longer seeking
for direction all alone,

but now hand in hand
with a friend.

You Have Always Been Here

-to and after Kelly Weber

I tried not to love you
but you've always been here
in the soft place
beneath the splintered wooden laths
that run under my plastered skin. No,
I shouldn't start out that way.
We shouldn't start with me
failing at this warmth caught
in my throat, this flush in my cheeks
smiling at the whirlpool
centered under tongue,
rushing down to belly, settling behind
skin you refuse to see.
If I take your arm as we
walk down the sidewalk,
what do we call this, love?
If you entwine your fingers
hold my hand to switch sides with me
so you are walking on the side of me
closest to the street,
an honorary protection you provide
against the world,
what do we call this love?
If we hug and I place my cheek to yours,
hold on a little longer
just to feel someone holding me,
just to be held,
is this the touch of friendship?
Do we call this platonic love?
If we grasp hands across the table as we talk
to emphasize a conversation,
do we call this an aromantic love?
If you rub my white cold fingers
to bring blood back into circulation
after I hold an iced coffee,
do we have to name this type of love?
Is what is between us
needing a name?
If you were always here
then are you not some central part of me,
some nerve

13

or blood or essential nutrient
I absorb when you are near?
I tried not to love you
but you have always been here,
always slept in my cells,
run electric currents
your palms lightning and breath.
I want to be your hand
show you the rest of my world
galaxies of mist evaporating,
call it platonic, call it love,
call it holding a place
you have always held.
Only know I have tried
I tried not to love you
but you have always,
always been here.

Knitting Scars

And you've healed and
there are scars that disfigure
but you are even okay
with the scars

Then someone comes along
and knits those scars together
to create something beautiful

and you are never the same
again

After Last Night

I will wait
but
if we keep feeling this desire for each other
I want to be able to touch you slowly
and enjoy it,
to do this before it becomes
a rushed bedraggled grasping
at each other
we can't control.

What you feel
it is natural
it is okay
it is normal
it is scary
it is vulnerable
it is intimate
it will change things
but it will deepen them

We are already like family
and we are adults
and can agree that
no matter what does happen
we will be okay with each other
even after it does.

Promise me
you will not run away
from what you feel…
but instead
run to me with it
and we will get through whatever we face
together.

Stay

I know
you are free to leave.

But if you leave
and I self-destruct:
do NOT
blame yourself.

I know
I don't deserve you.
I would be blessed
if you would only
stay.

Come Fly Away

They say time flies
when you're having fun
like some light and airy sparrow
taken to wing in spring
for the first time after a rainstorm
singing her heart out
at the sun

But they didn't tell me
when you left
the sparrow would fall to the ground
silent and heavy
like some rock tied to earth
by gravity
stone lifting the dirt to a hollow throat
and dry tongue
lips empty of song

My cheek searches for yours
my hand flutters into the open
alone
until that time
clock ticking
when sparrow will re-alight herself
song held out
wings catching the air
minutes seconds hours will press together
again
and you will be here

So come
come fly
come fly away
Come fly away with me

Elements

If you are the air
intuitively breathing the light
in dark times

then I am the water
reflecting that breath
into a thousand colors as I roam

But I am a fire
burning yearning in the deep
How will I not kiss you
the next time we meet?

Ground me
I'm floating to ashes
in your arms

Baseball

I am at the raised track in the YMCA,
prepared to walk
and distract myself
from thinking about you
the day before we are to see each other,
thinking the activity on the field below
will pull my mind away
from our conversation last night
when I notice they are playing baseball,
the subject we tried to talk
and think about to keep ourselves
away from each other's desire,
but the association with the sport
to progression in a couple's intimacy
prevented that,
and I am once again thinking
of standing on each base with you,
running slowly, taking time
with each part of your body,
and this makes me walk
even faster along the blue circle.
There is a woman running with the military
and she is struggling,
so I take myself out of my sensual imagination
with relief
to mentally cheer her on,
mumbling under my breath,
you can do it, keep going,
somehow telling myself the same thing.
When she completes her task
and collapses,
grasping her calves with a grimace,
my attention once more
trains onto lithe young college men
practicing below me,
a coach calling out
to a boy with your name,
and it is not their muscled skin
I want near me.
I walk so fast my steps
almost turn to jogging, and
when my time is done,

I am breathing hard,
hot-bodied and sweating,
still thinking of you.

Trust-fall

after P!nk

Oh, but I do
I do reach for you
through these miles
even though I said I wouldn't.

And yes,
though it would change what we have,
let's make the promise to say,
if this doesn't work,
that we still need our friendship,
and continue as that after,
a little closer and wiser
now that we know for sure.

If love is a longtime friend
whom you desire,
who is to say if it would truly change
what we already have;
or would it be acknowledging
what is there already?

The only thing I fear is the clock
running out of time.

You can still worship God
and have a partner:
let's be today's "Song
of Songs," shall we?

Let's call it a trust-fall:
when you are ready,
fall
and I will catch you;
I will never let you go.

Yes,
let's both . . .
why don't we fall?

Not From Here, Not For Long

Oh, you silly man!
She offers you a love
deeper than you can fathom
and you turn her down
for a belief so small
it is limited
to human constructs?

What have you done?

Of course she is different!
Haven't you figured out by now
why the universe can't hold her?
She is not of this world,
and neither is the love
she offers you.

Yet she believes herself
to be nothing,
a mere speck of light
in the vastness
of God herself.

We are not meant
to be alone;
God does not speak
with language in reply.

Come,
gather her into your arms.
Come know how God
answers your prayers.

The Empty Ring

Tonight on the indoor raised track
there are only two of us,
the other a middle-aged woman jogging,
because the Super Bowl has just started.
A few young boys playing soccer on the field
below me are cussing and teasing
with inappropriate comments
and I wonder where their parents are,
the slander towards gender and disability
and sexuality bothering me, so I turn
my mind elsewhere in search of distraction.

I think of yesterday,
when I passed a young man
on this same track who reminded me
of a friend of my son,
and I kept trying to figure out
if it was him, but I don't memorize
my son's friends' back ends,
so I never found out.
Yesterday on the field
they were also playing soccer, not baseball,
and I was grateful, because
as I walked these three lanes of blue
I was not supposed to be thinking of you.

I ended up doing it anyway.
We started our own game of baseball,
just barely touching first base
and then backing up,
returning to the friend zone,
but I think both of our minds are still
out there on the field—
though I wonder if our bodies will ever
make it past the wall you have built
for us.

You didn't want to want an old used
broken queer body you have known
all your life; you wanted a young fresh
new virgin angel to have your children,
even this late in your life.

I tell you, she doesn't exist.

You want to be ready, to have a sign
from God or something, but I tell you
I've never felt ready for anything in my life.
Even the blessings. Yet here they come.
We seem to be walking in circles
like the track I am on—
isn't it amazing that we pay someone
for the privilege to do this?
Walk in circles for our health?

I wear circles on my fingers—
each ring means something—
the one on my left ring finger
where a wedding band should be
acknowledges that I may never
find anyone who truly loves me
for who I am—
and that hurts every day.

I know my own choices for a partner
haven't worked out so well,
and when I had given up,
you came along,
so I thought God had given me you.
Maybe that was wrong, too.

But there are other ways of loving
that keep me alive for now.
Until then, this here is my empty ring.
Perhaps someday you will realize
no magical moment precedes love—
what is love, but a friend
to whom you can tell anything,
someone you want
in your life for the rest of your days,
and choose to remain faithful to?
Is that not what we have?

How long can someone love a wall?
How long can a ring hold the emptiness
away?
I keep walking my circles,
along three raised lanes of blue.

Queer

It's not that nobody wants me.

You want me.

You just don't want
to want me.

Your religion says
that I come from the devil.

That desire
for this body
this body with toppings
creating stirrings within
your body
is temptation
and desire is evil.

But didn't God create desire
to bring couples together?
And didn't God
create us all?
And didn't God command us
to love one another?

And aren't we all
under this skin
under our toppings

aren't we all human
and worthy of being touched,

of being loved?

Aren't we all worthy
of being wanted?

Oh that we could erase
these etchings
of earthy semantics.

Oh that I could transform
from nobody
to somebody
in your arms.

Help Me Let You Have This

This morning on the track
there are only two couples here with me,
this being a Sunday morning
and most people at church
to commune with their god,
but I can talk to mine anywhere,
and with every step I take
I am asking God
Help me let you have this
Help me let you have this
Help me let you have this
because I want to explain
that I am someone you tolerate
not someone you enjoy,
how your religion reminds you
all the time of your shortcomings and failures,
while my higher power
may have let me feel my powerlessness,
but built such an expanse of love
on top of that, I never had to go back
to the first step.
I wanted to explain
how I felt love for you, and sadness
that you can't love me for who I am
because your small limited male god
accepts only certain people,
forgives only certain sins,
lets only certain people in.
How disheartening and heavy;
do you not know your worth?
Do you not know the love
I have for you? The love in which
I have been immersed
and invited to share?
But today, tonight,
as I ask if I can even touch
your arm, your hand,
as you tolerate me
because you refuse to reconcile
the feelings you have for me,
I will say nothing.
I will know there may be a day

you finally leave.
A day your wall
will be so tall
I cannot get through.
But until then,
however I can,
I will still be loving you.

All This Love

I'm usually okay

but sometimes I cry

because I'm tired
of being alone.

Just once
I'd like to be enough
for someone.

To be their forever
for the rest
of our lives.

Oh, God:
am I to hold
all this love
for no one?

Goodbye, Love
Part I

I am driving home
the day after spending part of
an evening with you,
having slept the night at my friend's house,
so when you picked me up
it felt like an awkward
teenage date
and in a way, it was.

You didn't allow me
to touch you
and I tried to refrain from wanting
that physical closeness,
the intimacy that completes
any relationship.

You have accepted my alcoholism
and my mental illness, yet
hold my queerness out
as if it is some strange disease.

You can take almost all, yet
only a part of me.

Driving home, I am trying to think of a person
to accompany me to a Pride event,
one you refuse to attend.
The drive slides by swiftly,
only your name on my mind:
you were the one I wanted there with me.
But that is not to be.

The empty ring shall remain unmoved.
My feet will keep stepping to the refrain
Help me let you have this
and my higher power will hold it
as long as needed.

Hollow Heart

I am grieving right now
the loss of something
that never existed.

How can something empty
be so heavy
to carry?

Dealing with the anger I feel when you tell me you see me as a disposable untouchable ungodly temptress

I ripped you out of my poem today,
took down your picture—
both of them, the one at home AND the office,
rewrote the section of the poem
where we tell each other anything
and will last through everything.
Looks like we found something you hide
and something we won't last through.
Now a wall separates us,
one you built because your god sees me
as some menacing lower-tiered tempting aberration
pulled from a world you dare not see,
dare not touch, dare not engage with—
or it will blemish you, dirty you,
make you ungodly.
You can only see me from a distance
on rare occasions, text or call once in a while.
Yet we are still "friends". God forbid
you engage with us humans.
Ha. God forbid.
My god wouldn't.
My god is everywhere—is everything—
is and loves every atom ever spun in this universe.
We are built to interact and love and touch;
we are given desire to match and pair and share.
God gives in God's time—not ours.
We may not be ready, but God gives when God is ready.
It is our job to receive and react. In your way,
you did. By building a wall.
So I do not break down or climb over.
I do not chase.
I breathe. I love. I walk on.

Doing the Dishes After the Time Change

The time changed last night,
causing us to spring forward

an hour, leaving me a bit discombob-
ulated, and I have just lost my friend,

not from death, but for your own reasons,
maybe because I love too much,

but this finds me staring out the kitchen window
on a Sunday morning in March,

doing dishes in my house alone,
crying, my tears joining the dishwater in the sink.

The song "Come Cryin' to Me" is playing in the background
but I can't come crying to you anymore,

can't tell you how this feels,
because you won't care.

You won't care that I'm writing another poem
about heartbreak, about grief.

I will cry more than "One Solitary Tear"
and you won't care.

But I will walk past the sign my daughter made
for me, and like it says, "Nevertheless She Persisted,"

I will persist.
I will persist because this will pass.

I will persist because my body will go through the motions
until it hurts just a little less.

I will persist until
you are another scar on this mangled heart.

I will persist because there are others
who do love me. And you will not care,

but the tears I cry will swirl down the drain,
will leave me clean as they join the dishwater,

disappearing, becoming another memory
that causes me to sigh,

another memory I wish would have ended
differently,

another memory I fold into the pages of my journey
and move on.

**

Coda:
And then the song "This Is Me" plays,
and I put on the dress with the colors of the sky,

and I become a cloud,
and float to the friends who love me

just as I am today.

**

Maybe someday I will see you
in the colors of the sunrise.

Eagle, Cloud, Whisker: I Just Miss You

Last Thursday, two bald eagles circled in the blue sky
above me as I drove home in the subdued afternoon.
The optimist in me believed they were a mated pair,
hunting together. Even the lone eagle needs a partner.

Today, I wrapped the cottony fluff of a sherpa jacket
around me under my raincoat to feel
as if I was walking around in a cloud.
It reminded me of the time I held your arm last winter
and we walked downtown to get coffee;
I was floating at your side.

Tomorrow, I will step over the remains of a stem
and observe that it resembles the whisker of a cat—
with it the plant is reaching to feel the world,
brush the air, just like any feline would.
The optimist in me will see their similarities—
both capable of feeling.

Last Thursday, the optimist in me
could see our conversation on the phone
as a reaching out, a connection
despite our distance, our lack of touch.

Today, the rain taps out the melody of longing,
of loneliness, of despondency, of emptiness;
the cloud that hangs between us.

Tomorrow: will I ever have a tomorrow
when I will feel you again?
Wrap my arm in yours?
Can you sense the sorrow across the miles?

Yesterday's eagle, today's cloud, tomorrow's whisker;
hunting a partner, floating in rain, feeling:
I guess this is all just a way of saying
I miss you.

Bear Minimum

Bare minimum. As in the
smallest amount acceptable—
nothing less. Bare, as in skin,
as in that organ that covers you,
as in the nerve-filled sack cloth
that holds bones and muscle
from exposure, that flakes when dry,
that bleeds when cut.
Bare minimum—nothing less than
the body you were born in,
the cells that are fully replaced
every seven years or so—
meaning if you wait too long,
no cell on my body will remember
touching you, remember seeing you.
Change the bare minimum to
bear minimum—bear, as in
unbearable, this empty feeling,
this sand burr in my heart—change it
and it is merely bear minimum,
or smallest creature that dwells
in caves and forests, as in bear cub,
or baby bear—the bear when it is born—
the smallest it will ever be.
Bear minimum, as in sun bear,
the smallest of its kind,
tiniest species of the family Ursidae,
which is funny because the sun
is the biggest star in our sky.
Minimum, as in our relationship now,
only talking, only texting,
only at a distance—reaching a maximum
across these miles with voice
and thumbs and words.
Heart locked with this burr studded
inside, ripping a hole, bare minimum rope
tied around bleeding muscle
to keep it from jumping out of this skin,
this bare skin,
wanting to touch,
to find you again.

Like the Willow

It is the first warm Saturday morning of Spring
and I am performing a chore usually done in the Fall:
raking my leaves into the compost pile.

I am also picking up sticks from the wind storms
that beat them from surrounding trees.
Dealing with the dead, the detritus of the living.

Creating nourishment out of discards,
food for a beginning
where there once was an ending.

Spring is showing her own beginnings around me:
moths are arriving at the porch light with my lace wings,
buds greening and expanding, grass fluttering hello.

I rake three wheelbarrows full of twigs from under the willow,
this Being coated in neon green baby leaves,
a tree that sheds even when it is trimmed,

its heart trapped and protected within hardness,
too full to keep everything to itself,
this shedding a way of giving, of releasing, of letting go,
of sighing in the storm.

Tomorrow I will travel with my friend for our poetry reading
and you will be there,
and I will wonder where your heart is.

Like the willow,
your heart is protected under hardness,
irretrievable and unreachable.

Like the willow,
my heart is full to bursting,
needing to shed and give and share.

Tomorrow, as I read and look at you,
I will wonder if there is still time,
while our hearts still beat in proximity,

for them to find each other,
to rake the life into this love,
to find a way beneath the resistance to truly live.

Or will my heart that reaches for you fill to bursting
and need to shed, like the willow, need to let go,
and will one of those things that goes be you?

After the reading we will not speak
and as the darkness lights the stars
and the moon stretches his arms,

cradling all the loneliness,
I will wonder where your heart is
and if my heart is too much,

my burst of neon coral love
too bright for this spring day,
my touch too electric for your nerves.

Will you hold on, or,
like the willow,
will you let go?

Goodbye, Love
Part II

And I will let go,
even though
I don't know when I will see you again.

I will let go
as I drive away from you
until you can take all of me.

Goodbye, love.

Is it okay if I cry?

The highway to home stretches
out in front of me.

I don't know how this story ends.

About the Author

Julie S. Paschold (Tansy Julie the Soaring Eagle) (she/ they) is a poet and artist from Nebraska. They have their BS and MS in agronomy from the University of Nebraska at Lincoln. Their first book, Horizons (Atmosphere Press) is a collection of poetry honoring soil, one of our nonrenewable resources. Julie has been published in a wide range of publications. Their poem "Multitudes of Blue Arrows" was a semi-finalist in the first Kate Sommers Memorial Prize in 2023, and two of their chapbooks won honorable mention in contests by Writer's Digest in 2021 and 2022. They are a published book with the international Human Library Organization. For more, read their blog on https://medium.com/@jpaschold or their author website at https://jpaschold.blogspot.com/ .